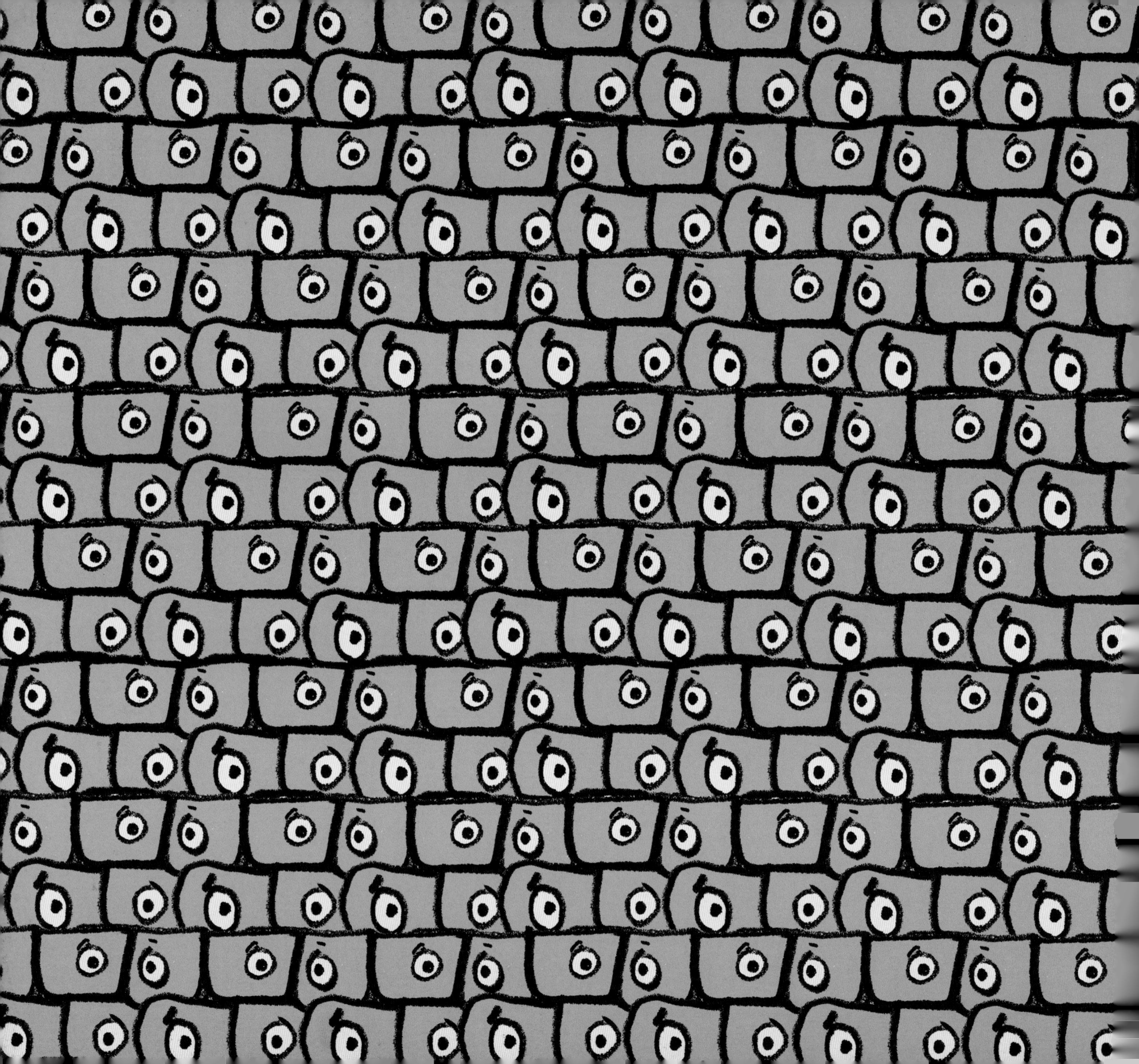

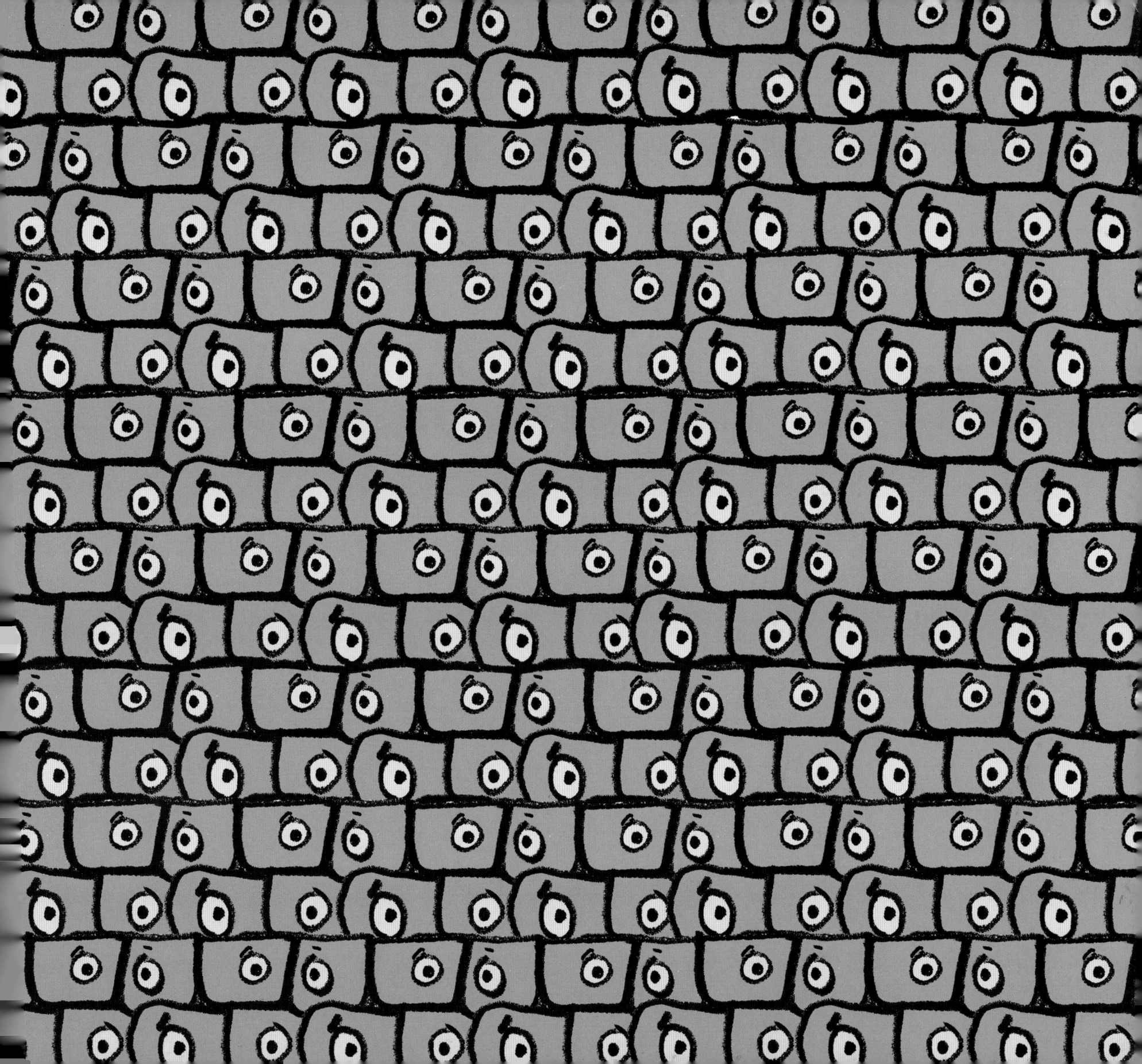

This book is dedicated to the wonderful Alisons

There are three more books in this series and they tell you just about everything you need to know about the whole world – and even the stars.

THE STORY OF STARS
THE STORY OF EVERYTHING
THE STORY OF THINGS

Find out much more about Neal Layton on his website: www.neallayton.co.uk

First published in Great Britain in 2023 by Wren & Rook

HB ISBN: 978 1 5263 6265 0
PB ISBN: 978 1 5263 6264 3

10 8 6 4 2 1 3 5 7 9

MIX
Paper from responsible sources
FSC® C104740

FSC
www.fsc.org

Wren & Rook
An imprint of Hachette Children's Group
Part of Hodder & Stoughton
Carmelite House, 50 Victoria Embankment, London EC4Y 0DZ

An Hachette UK Company
www.hachette.co.uk
www.hachettechildrens.co.uk

Printed in China

NEAL LAYTON

THE BIG STORY OF BEING ALIVE

A Brilliant Book About What Makes You EXTRAORDINARY

wren
&rook

When you go out in the street
look at all the people you can see.

There are lots of them.
And no one looks quite the same.

But all these very different people have one thing in common . . . they are all ALIVE.

Bleep!

Except this guy.
He is definitely not alive.

YOU are alive too.

Which is great, because if you weren't alive, you wouldn't be sitting looking at this book wondering what I'm talking about. I think being alive is TOTALLY AMAZING.

Are you alive?
Then this book could be for you!

It's a story about the MOST amazing thing in the WHOLE universe, LIFE. It's a BIG important story and you are part of it too ...

From the cells that our bodies are built of to how we grow and how babies are made, this is the story of what makes you YOU.

THE BIG STORY OF

NEAL LAYTON

THE BIG STORY OF BEING ALIVE

Discover how amazing living things YOU grow

A flying fly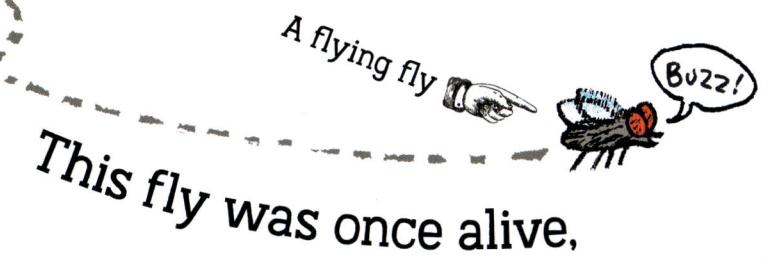

This fly was once alive,

Not flying fly

and sadly now it is not.

EEEK! PLEASE WATER ME!

And this flower. If it doesn't get enough Sun and water, it will go brown and wither away . . . and die.

But what about this stone.
Is it alive? Was it ever alive?

A stone

So what does it mean to say that something is ALIVE?

Scientists, philosophers and doctors find it very difficult to agree on what makes some things living and other things not.

But there are some things that *EVERYTHING* alive has in common:

They are CELLULAR

They GROW

They can REPRODUCE

But what does THAT mean?

Let's start with CELLULAR. It's a BIG word, but it all has to do with tiny things called cells.

Cells come in different shapes and sizes.

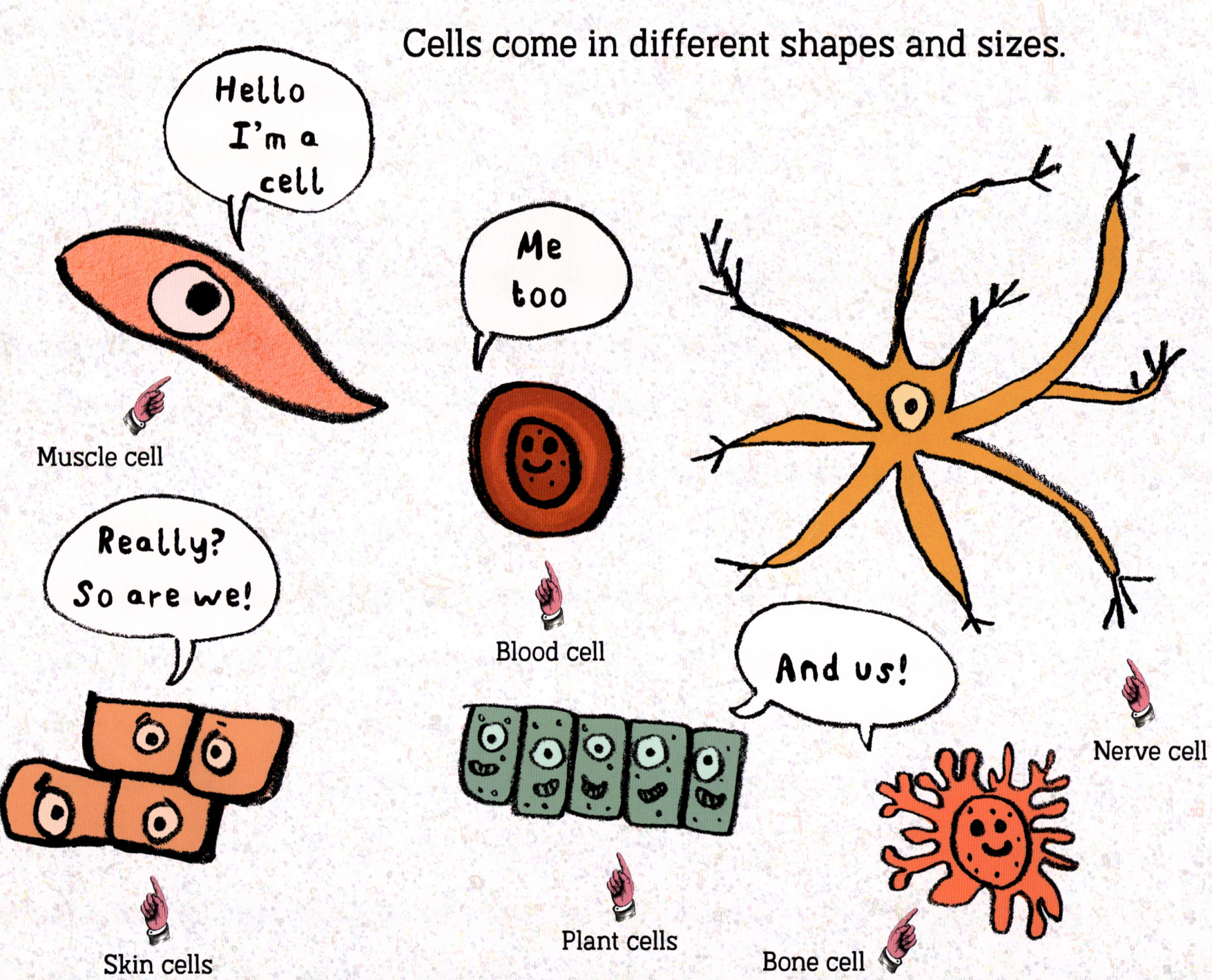

Hello I'm a cell

Me too

Really? So are we!

And us!

Muscle cell

Blood cell

Nerve cell

Skin cells

Plant cells

Bone cell

You, me and everybody started life as two cells.

One of them came from your mum . . .

YOUR MUM'S
← CELL

and the other came from your dad.

YOUR DAD'S ↗
MUCH SMALLER CELL

BUT what IS a CELL?

Cells are the tiny building blocks that make up ALL LIVING THINGS.

LIVING THINGS (MADE OF CELLS)

NOT LIVING THINGS (NOT MADE OF CELLS)

Some tiny organisms, such as bacteria and yeast, only have one cell. But large plants and animals have many BILLIONS of cells. And grown-up human beings are made up of more than 75,000,000,000,000 (75 trillion) cells.

Large animal

Screen connected to microscope

Grown-up human made of lots of cells

Microscope for looking at small things

Bacteria

Yeast

Large plant

Most cells are really small.
Much, much smaller than this dot.

But, although they are tiny, cells are REALLY clever
and packed with very important stuff.

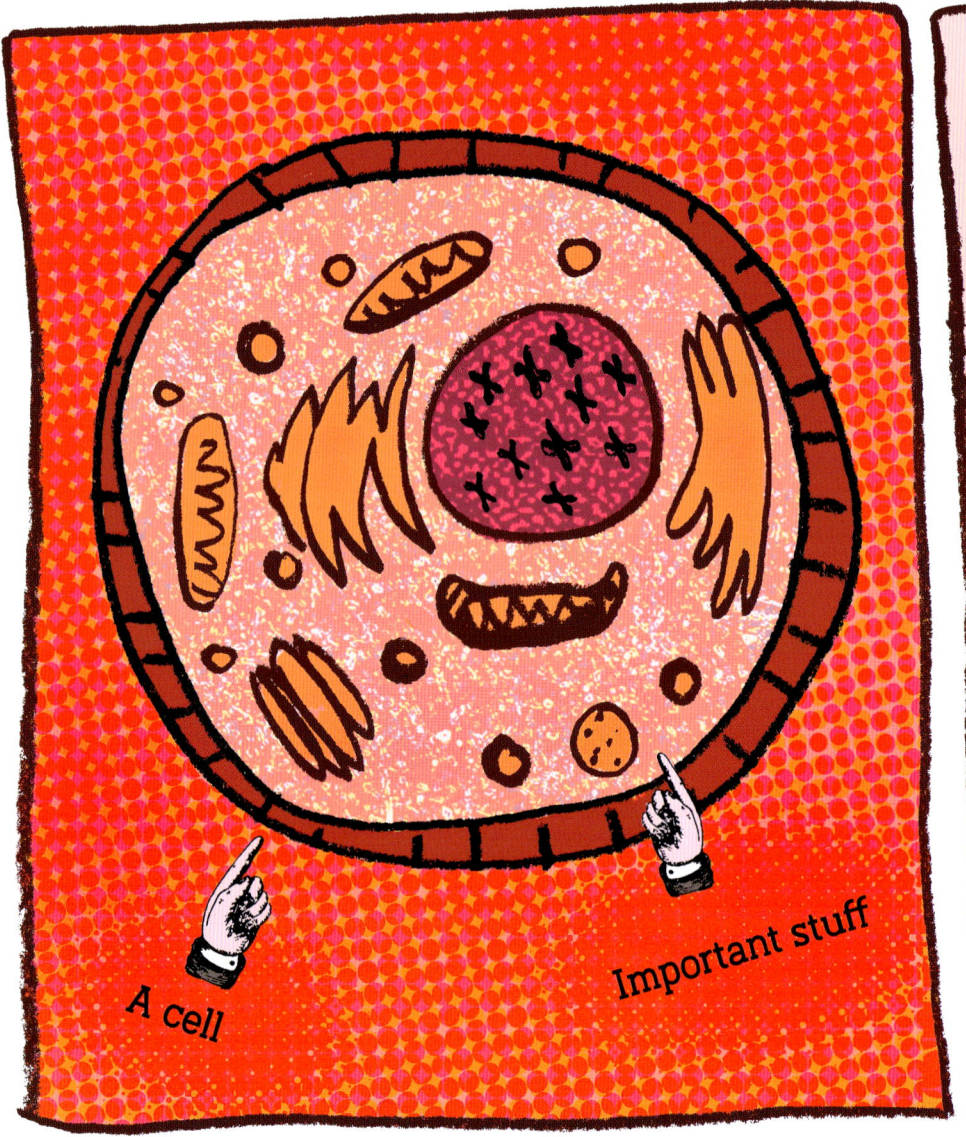

A cell

Important stuff

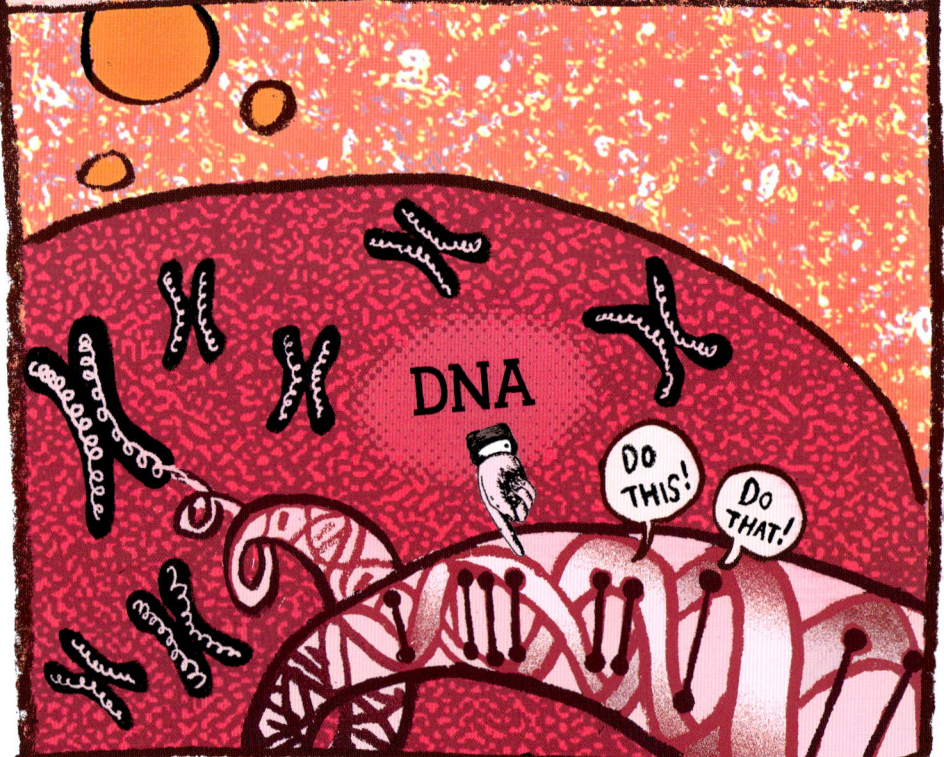

Hidden inside the important
stuff are special instructions
called DNA that tell the cells
what to do.

DNA

DO THIS!

DO THAT!

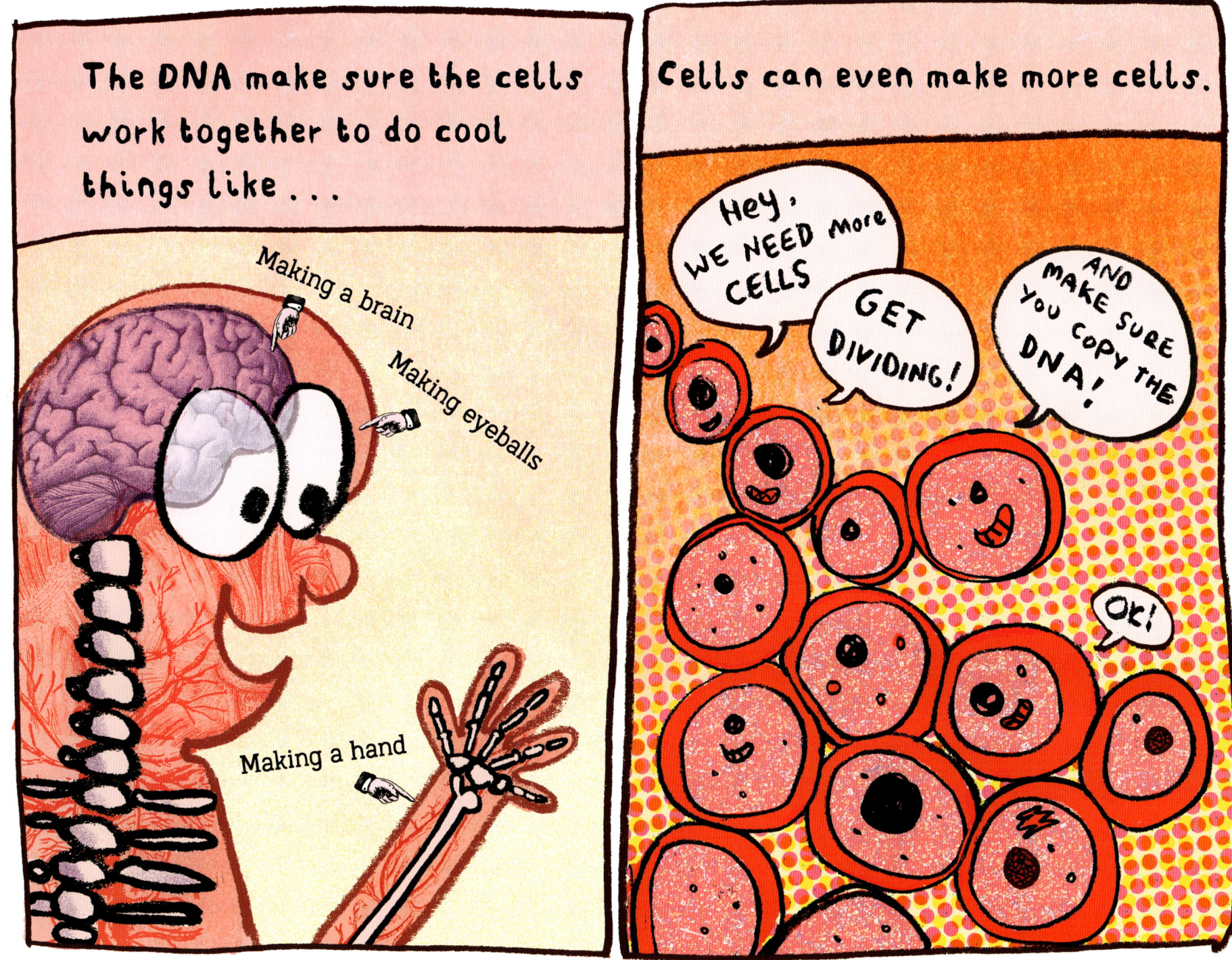

Which brings us to the second part of being alive . . .

growing!

Without cells you could not have grown into the wonderful human being that you are!

Do you want to hear something REALLY cool?

If you fall over and graze your knee, healthy cells can even GROW NEW SKIN.

This is very useful as otherwise we would need lots of sticky plasters.

Cells are also behind . . . REPRODUCTION!
Which is how alive things make more of themselves.

Things reproducing

Thing growing

Thing growing

Reproduction keeps our planet brimming with life!

All alive things get old and die in the end. So, if they don't reproduce, there wouldn't be any more plants or insects or animals or fish or birds or humans!

Things growing

Things reproducing

Things reproducing

Thing growing

You're probably wondering how YOU grew from those two cells from your mum and your dad.

When the cells got together in your mum's womb, IMPORTANT things started happening. They shared their DNA, which made instructions for a NEW human being, YOU!

Then they made a whole load of new cells.
Two cells became four, then eight . . .
Every cell had its own important job to do.

Grow a heart

Make some blood

And so, a little baby started to grow.

Very early babies are called embryos!

After three weeks, the baby
is the size of a grain of rice.

At five weeks, it's about the size of a pea.

But it grows . . .

and it grows . . .

and it GROWS . . .

After nine months, it has a brain. A heart. Two lungs. Lots of bones. And probably about 26,000,000,000 cells!

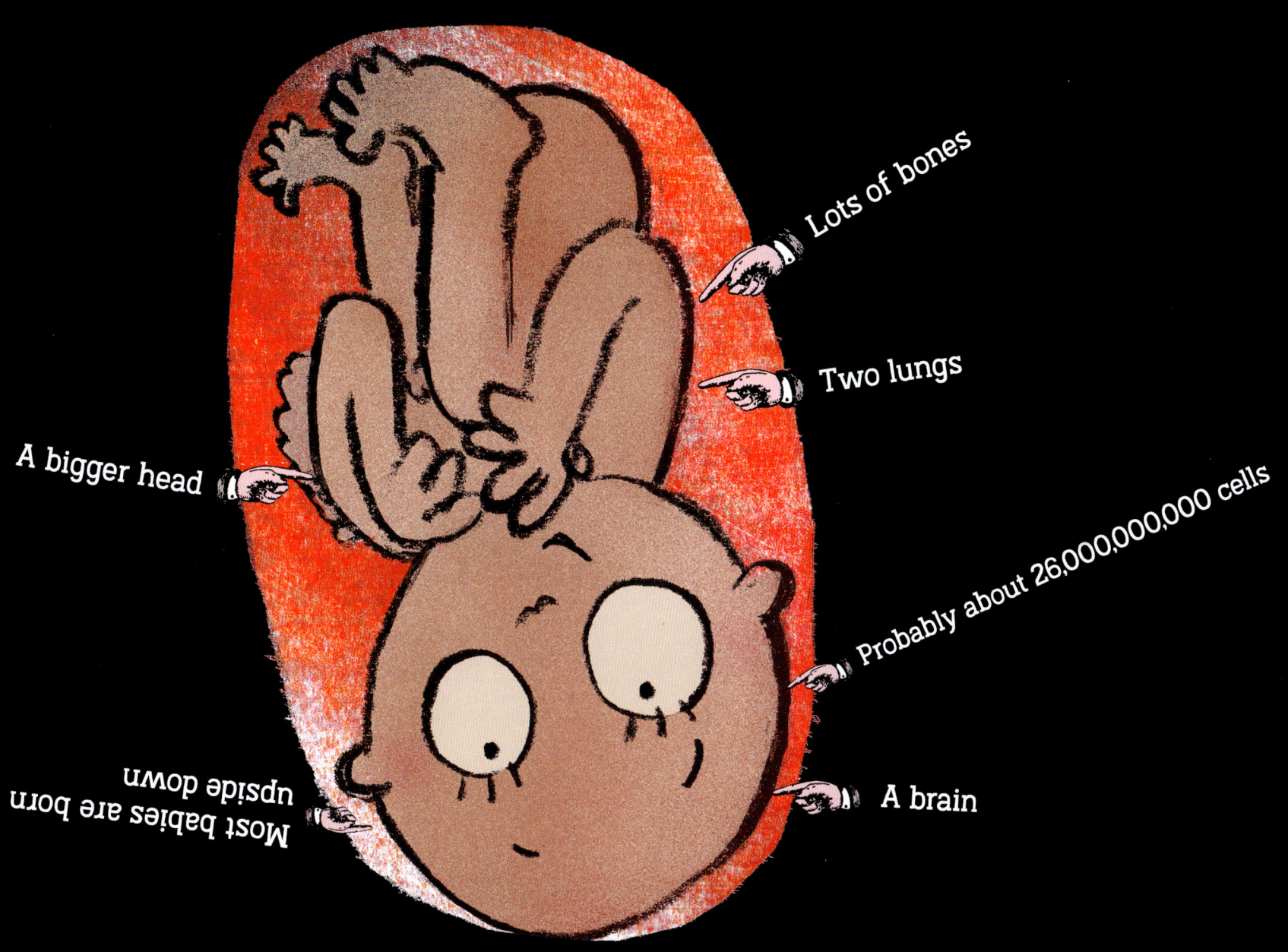

Lots of bones

Two lungs

A bigger head

Probably about 26,000,000,000 cells

Most babies are born upside down

A brain

The baby doesn't need the womb anymore. So . . .

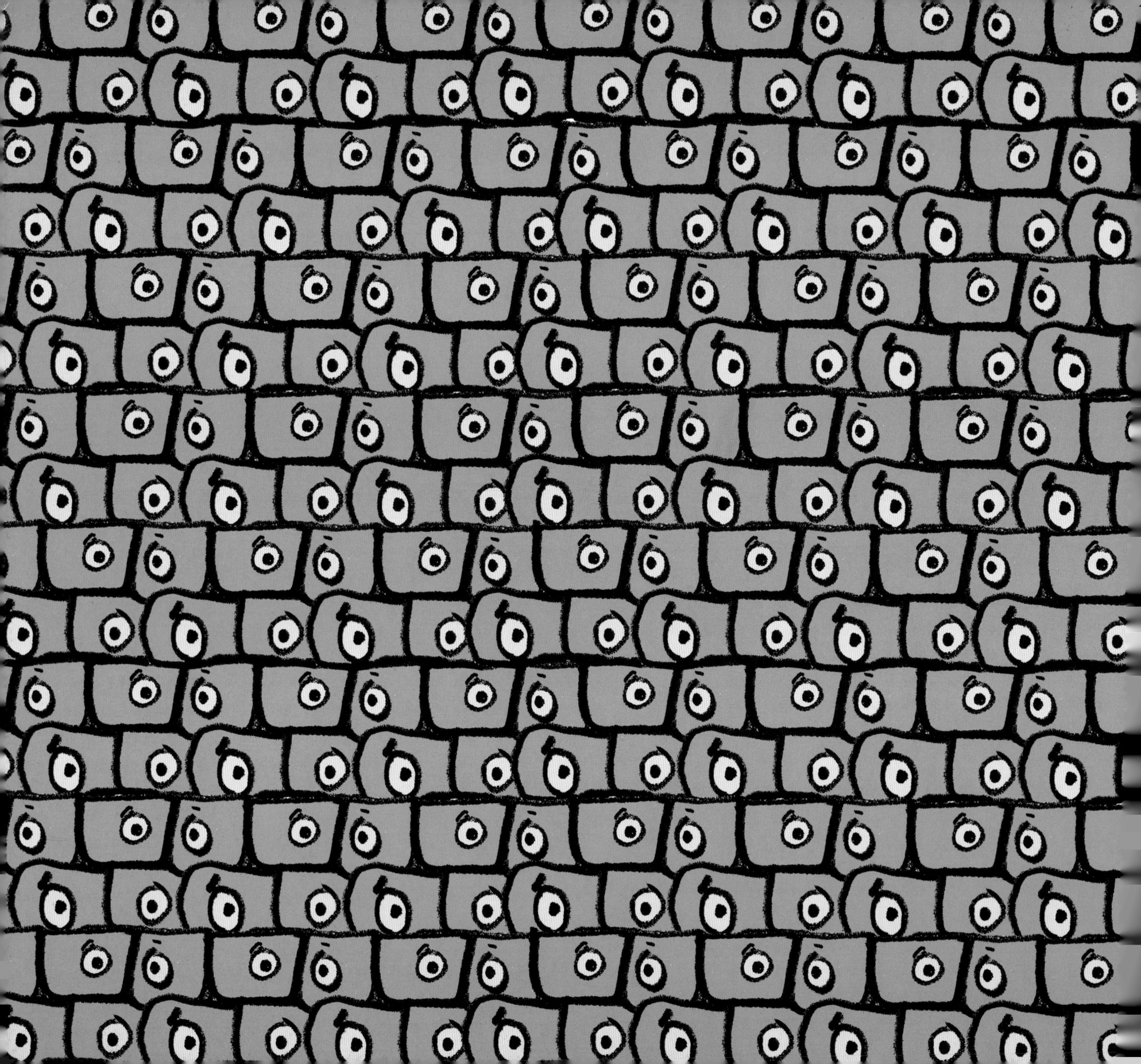

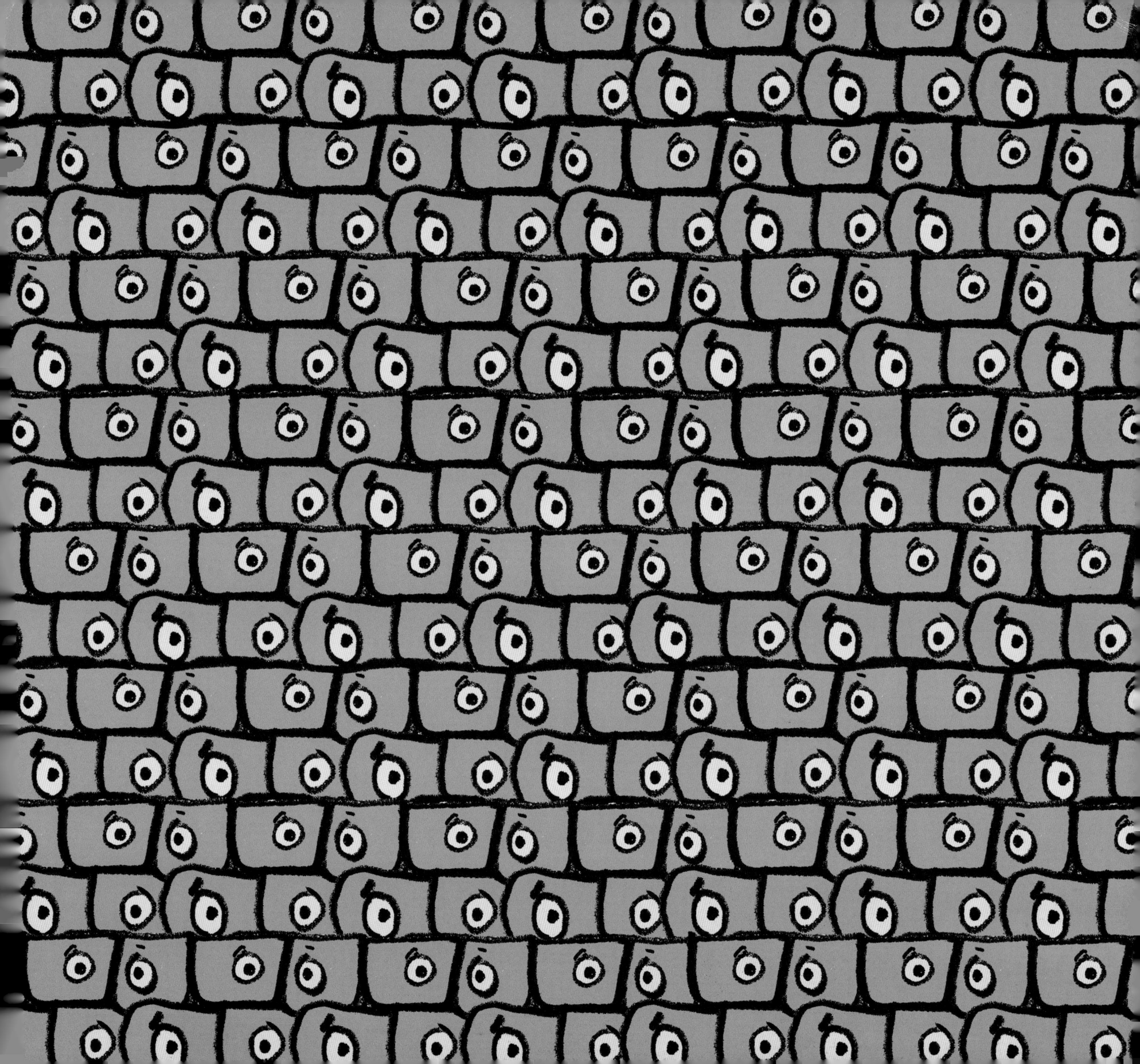